1019

920
BAK

Baker, Susan

Explorers of North America

$18.60

DATE			
SEP 3 0 1992			
NOV 02 1992			

BAKER & TAYLOR BOOKS

EXPLORERS OF NORTH AMERICA

Indians attack a covered wagon train on its way west, as it crosses a river.

TALES OF COURAGE

□

EXPLORERS OF NORTH AMERICA

□

BY SUSAN BAKER

Illustrated by Andrew Howat

□

STECK-VAUGHN
LIBRARY
A Division of Steck-Vaughn Company

**Published in the United States in 1990
by Steck-Vaughn Co., Austin, Texas,**
a subsidiary of National Education Corporation.

A Cherrytree Book

Designed and produced by
A S Publishing

Photographs by Western Americana
Maps by Gordon Davidson

Library of Congress Cataloging-in-Publication Data

Baker, Susan, 1961–
    Explorers of North America / by Susan Baker ; illustrated by
Andrew Howat.
        p.   cm. — (Tales of courage)
    Summary: Brief descriptions of North American explorers and their
accomplishments up to the time of the Gold Rush. Includes Columbus,
the Pilgrims, and Daniel Boone.
    ISBN 0-8114-2752-8
    1. Explorers—North America—Biography—Juvenile literature.
2. North America—Discovery and exploration—Juvenile literature.
3. Pioneers—North America—Biography—Juvenile literature.
4. Frontier and pioneer life—North America—Juvenile literature.
[1. Explorers. 2. Frontier and pioneer life. 3. North America–
–Discovery and exploration.] I. Howat, Andrew. II. Title.
III. Series.
E36.B35   1990
917.304′092′2—dc20
[B]
[920]   89-26364
                                                               CIP
                                                                AC

Printed in Italy by New Interlitho
Bound in the United States by Lake Book, Melrose Park, IL
1 2 3 4 5 6 7 8 9 0 IL 94 93 92 91 90

▫ CONTENTS ▫

□ THE NEW WORLD □

The vast continent of North America presented so many obstacles to the early settlers that it defied exploration to all but a few brave people.

The fifteenth century was the age of discovery. Spain and Portugal were the world's most powerful nations. Trade flourished between cities and states, and the great nations sent sailors to discover new lands and find new and quicker routes to the rich lands of the East. One such sailor was Christopher Columbus. In 1492, he set sail westward with three small wooden ships across the "sea with no known shore." He hoped to reach Japan, but few people believed he would

succeed: it was a foolish and dangerous idea. As weeks went by, his crew grew more and more afraid. Then, after 33 days at sea, they sighted land.

The finding of America

They had reached the West Indies, which Columbus described as a tropical paradise. He called the dark-skinned people who greeted him "Indians" because he believed he had reached India. These native Americans were indeed descendants

Columbus lands triumphantly on the island of San Salvador in the West Indies, after five weeks on the "Sea of Darkness" with only the unknown ahead.

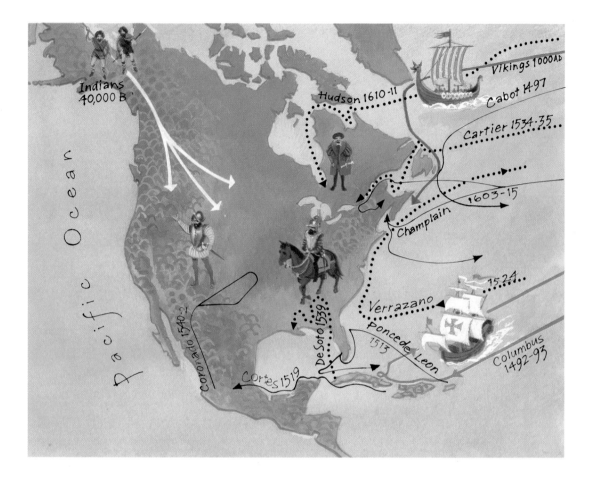

The map shows various explorers' routes including:
- Indians 40,000 B.C.
- Vikings 1000 A.D.
- Cabot 1497
- Hudson 1610-11
- Cartier 1534-35
- Champlain 1603-15
- Verrazano 1524
- Ponce de Leon 1513
- Columbus 1492-93
- De Soto 1539
- Coronado 1540-2
- Cortes 1519
- Pacific Ocean

of people from Asia, people who had traveled through northern Europe and crossed into North America many thousands of years before, at a time when a land bridge connected the two continents. The wandering tribes were the first to explore America. The tribes that reached Central and South America built fine cities and collected gold and other treasure.

News of Columbus's discovery spread through Europe, and more people set out to follow his westward route to the "Indies." Eventually people began to realize that these new islands were not part of Asia. According to Amerigo Vespucci,

The ancestors of the Indians traveled to – and through – America on foot. Later, Europeans came by sea, first the Vikings who did not stay, then others who did.

they were part of a new world, a world that people named America in his honor.

The race to claim land

The next discovery the Europeans made in America was gold, and this brought many more adventurers, including the Spanish conquistadors (conquerors). They struggled through the hot, fever-ridden rain forests and scorching deserts of South and Central America in search

of gold. They were led by tough, ruthless men. Among them was Cortes, the first European to see the Pacific Ocean. He fought terrible battles with the Aztecs in his conquest of Mexico. Another was Pizarro who triumphed over the courageous Inca people of Peru.

The Portuguese also claimed lands in South America. It was their great navigator Magellan who found a passage to the Pacific around the tip of South America.

Eager for more gold, the Spanish pushed northward with their armies. Hernando De Soto traveled up through Florida and came upon the Mississippi River. Francisco de Coronado rode across the scorching southwest desert to the Grand Canyon.

The Indians grew to hate the invaders who stole not only their gold but also

With few tools and weapons, the Pilgrims had to hunt, clear land, plant crops, hew timber for buildings, and coexist with the natives.

their land. They brought fatal diseases with them and captured many natives to use as slaves. For centuries afterward, Europeans who emigrated to America had to fight off hostile Indians to protect their settlements. Those who ventured beyond the settlements to explore went fearing for their lives.

Following the Vikings
Still seeking a westward route to the Indies, other navigators sailed to North America in the hope of finding a "Northwest Passage." Unknowingly, they followed the route taken by the Europeans

The first colonies

For many years much of North America was under French rule, but colonies of English settlers were growing rapidly.

The countries of Europe were constantly at war. During these troubled times, many people took the opportunity of escaping from Europe and making a fresh start in the new country. Hundreds risked the dangerous journey across the Atlantic in small, wooden ships. Some came to seek their fortunes. Others, like the Pilgrims, came to escape religious intolerance in Europe.

They found the New World astonishing but daunting. It was a land of opportunity, but only those with great strength, courage, and determination survived its perils.

Hungry for land

The new continent was a vast land of forests, mountains, plains, and deserts. The early settlers clung to the coasts. The great mountains rising to the west of them were the limit of their sight.

Fearless fur traders ventured into the forests and set up trading posts. There was fierce competition among them, and among the European nations from which they came. Hungry for land and power, the French sought new trading routes. In 1682, Sieur de La Salle found the mouth of the Mississippi and claimed the whole of the Mississippi valley for France. He called it Louisiana, after the French king, Louis XIV.

On the east coast, towns grew as more settlers from Europe arrived. The English, already at loggerheads with the French, clashed with Dutch farmers and traders over claims to territory. As time went on the conflicts grew worse.

Gun in hand, Captain John Smith "arrests" an Indian chief, armed only with a bow and arrow. Smith's skilled leadership and prowess often prevented bloodshed.

who had found America 500 years before Columbus. These were the Vikings, remarkable seafaring warriors from Scandinavia, who had crossed the Atlantic in longships and settled for a time on the coast of Newfoundland. Among them were Eric the Red and his son Leif Ericsson.

Their northern route was followed by John Cabot, an Italian who sailed under the English flag. Other countries in Europe were eager to claim land in the New World, too. In 1535 Jacques Cartier explored the huge gulf leading to the St. Lawrence River, claiming land for France.

By the mid 1700s England, France, the Netherlands, Spain, and Portugal had divided up America between them, or at least what they knew of America. Most of the land was unexplored, except by its native population. They had lived for centuries in the forests, on the plains, in the mountains, and in the deserts, each tribe adapting its way of life to its surroundings. They grew corn and gathered nuts and berries. On the plains, they hunted buffalo, shooting them with arrows. In the forests, they shot game. The Europeans callously disregarded their rights. They had power over the native Americans because they had superior weapons – guns. When it suited them, they gave guns to the Indians in exchange for their support in wars.

The French and Indian Wars

Great Britain now had 13 colonies along the east coast of America. To the south were the Spanish and to the north and west were the French. In a long, drawn out war, lasting seven years, the French (who had purchased the support of the Indians) were finally defeated and the English received Canada and the northern colonies. All Louisiana west of the Mississippi was given to Spain.

The struggle for independence

As the number of settlers on the east coast grew, the competition for land increased. People who found unoccupied land could "stake a claim" to it. Despite the dangers they knew (and many they didn't), the braver souls ventured farther inland. Explorers risked their lives on the freezing mountains and foaming rivers in defiance of the Indians.

By 1760 the population of the British colonies had risen to more than 1,500,000. They traded with the British who sailed into Boston and other ports with cargoes of tea, china, cloth, tools, and weapons. The British army protected the colonies, and for this the colonists paid taxes to the British king. But by now, they felt themselves to be Americans. They could fend for themselves. They owed neither allegiance – nor taxes – to a king they had never seen. The struggle for independence had begun.

The colonists made their Declaration of Independence in 1776. The British opposed them, and the American Revolutionary War began. It lasted until 1783 when the United States of America became a free nation, and the British army sailed home.

Opening up the West

In 1803 the United States purchased the territory of Louisiana from the French (who now held it again, but needed money to fight their battles in Europe). The United States was suddenly double in size. Little was known about the new territory or the Indians who lived there, so the United States government sent out official expeditions to survey and map the miles of unknown country they laid claim to. It was an enormous task and the courageous men who completed it rightly became heroes.

From the air, today's travelers can see what the explorers of North America faced on the ground: in the north, freezing tundra and thick forests; in the south, deserts and swamps; in the center, vast plains and broad rivers; and running the length of the country, huge mountain chains.

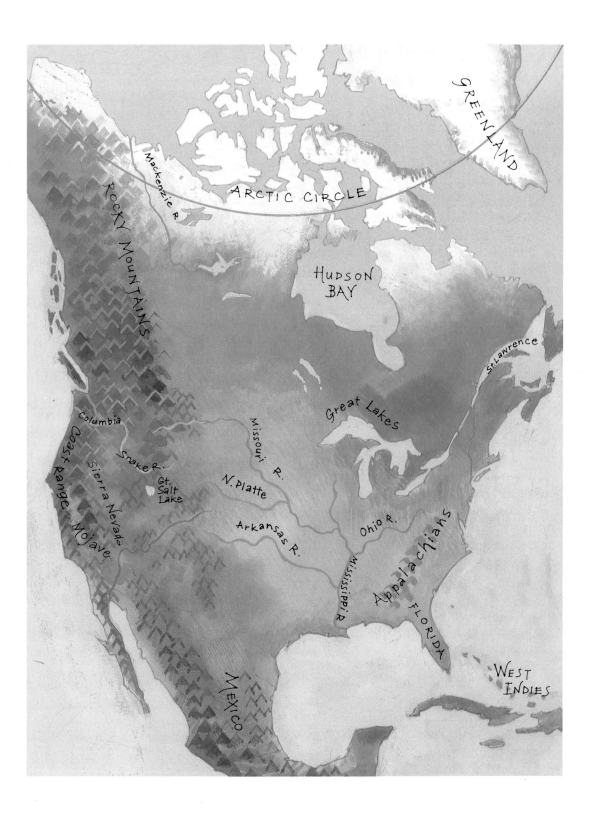

GREENLAND

Mackenzie R.

ARCTIC CIRCLE

ROCKY MOUNTAINS

HUDSON BAY

St. Lawrence

Great Lakes

Columbia

Snake R.

Sierra Nevada

Coast Range

Mojave

Gt. Salt Lake

Missouri R.

N. Platte

Arkansas R.

Ohio R.

Mississippi R.

Appalachians

FLORIDA

MEXICO

WEST INDIES

THE NORTHWEST PASSAGE

Magellan proved that there was a southwest passage to the East. John Cabot died in an attempt to find a passage to the north. Even so, a variety of adventurers followed him through the treacherous icy waters of the Arctic.

As soon as he was old enough to command a ship, Sebastian Cabot determined to continue his father's search for a sea route to China. In 1508 he set sail with two ships. The huge icebergs that drift down from the Arctic could easily have crushed them to pieces. Cabot sailed right into the mouth of what is now Hudson Bay. This, he felt certain, was the Northwest Passage. But his terrified crew refused to sail any farther and they turned back.

JACQUES CARTIER

In 1534 Jacques Cartier set off to look for gold in the New World. He sailed west and found himself at the mouth of a huge river, which he named the St. Lawrence. He wondered if this wide gulf could lead to the Northwest Passage.

Returning on a second voyage, he sailed up the river. Instead of finding Asia, he found an Indian settlement (the future city of Montreal). With great skill and courage Cartier made peace with the Iroquois Indians. In 1541, he made a third voyage, this time to found a colony. Trapped by the winter freeze, he spent the winter at another Indian village that later became Quebec.

Life was extremely hard and dangerous for these first French settlers. The winter climate was harsher than any they had known. Hostile Indians made brutal attacks on them. Shortages of fresh food brought death and disease. In the end, they decided to abandon the settlement before more lives were lost.

SAMUEL DE CHAMPLAIN

Nearly 80 years later, Samuel de Champlain led an expedition from France. He discovered the vast inland seas known as the Great Lakes, and must have been one of the first Europeans to see the staggering spectacle of Niagara Falls.

In 1608 Champlain set up a fur trading post at Quebec. This became the first permanent settlement, but of the 24 settlers, only 8 survived their first bitterly cold winter. Severe weather was not the only problem. The settlers were to live by hunting and trapping in territory that was already settled. The Iroquois jealously guarded their hunting grounds.

Champlain's settlement at Quebec was also threatened by the English. Helped by the Iroquois, they laid siege to the settlement, cutting off precious supplies to starve the French out. Eventually the settlement surrendered and Champlain was taken prisoner. But he never gave up hope. On his release, he returned to Quebec, newly regained by the French, and became its governor. He became known as the Father of New France – or Canada, as the Indians called their lands beside the St. Lawrence.

The citizens of Bristol turned out in strength to give a grand send-off to John and Sebastian Cabot as they set sail for North America in 1497.

□ HENRY HUDSON □

In 1610, the English explorer Henry Hudson sailed into the great bay that was named after him. Determined to find a route to China, Hudson kept his ship *Discovery* in the bay, locked in the pack ice, all winter. Extreme cold, hunger, disease, and fear of the unknown made conditions for the sailors unbearable. At last the spring thaw began and the ship broke free of the winter ice. But it was too late. The crew was mutinous. Three days later, the sailors set Hudson, his young son, and seven loyal sailors adrift in a small, open boat with no provisions. They were never seen again.

□ PASSAGE OVERLAND □

The far north of North America is extremely cold, hard terrain. In 1772, Samuel Hearne, a fur trader and explorer employed by the Hudson's Bay Company, made his way from Hudson Bay across the frozen tundra to the Arctic Ocean. He was the first white man to make the journey.

The first white man to cross from the Atlantic coast to the Pacific was a Scottish settler named Alexander Mackenzie. He found his way from the Great Slave Lake to the Arctic Ocean. With a small band of friends and Indian guides, he followed the course of the river that now bears his name. He himself called it the "river of disappointment." He had expected it to lead him to the Pacific and it had let him down.

Mackenzie was discouraged but not defeated. Three years later, in 1793, he tried again. This time he followed the Peace River farther south. This led him across the Rockies to the Pacific, some 11 years before Lewis and Clark's historic journey. He had proved that there was a Northwest Passage – overland.

□ INTREPID FUR TRAPPERS □

When the vast hunting grounds of the New World were discovered, fur became the height of fashion in Europe. Everyone wanted a stylish beaver hat.

The great rivers and forests of North America teemed with beaver and other animals. Fur trappers and traders explored deep into Indian territory and endured freezing temperatures during the long, hard winters. The beaver's fur grows long and thick in winter, to help it survive the cold, and the longer the fur the higher the price it would fetch.

The hunters and trappers lived in rough shelters or built huts from logs. The trappers copied the Indians, making tough, warm clothes out of skins to replace their flimsy European ones. They ventured deep inland along the rivers.

The beaver's beautiful fur was used to make felt top hats, as well as warm winter coats.

Like the Indians, they traveled swiftly by canoe down the foaming waterways. In canoes they were vulnerable not only to rocks and rapids, but also to the Indians who watched them from vantage points. In any narrow gorge, an Indian marksman could easily fire on them.

Paths through the forest were equally frightening. The only way a man on a horse laden with furs could get through the forest was by using an Indian trail. Lying in ambush, the Indians simply waited to shoot down the hunters and steal their furs. Often the Indians would leave a warning to others. Many a trapper came across the mutilated corpse of a friend. The Indians hated the intruders; often they tortured their victims and took their scalps as trophies.

There was so much trapping, by settlers and by Indians who sold furs to the traders, that in some places the animals became scarce. New hunting grounds had to be found so that fashionable folk could still have their beaver hats.

□ ROBERT STUART □

In 1810, Jacob Astor decided to send a fur-trading team directly to the Pacific Northwest by sea. The members of the expedition made the dangerous voyage around Cape Horn, South America, and landed near the mouth of the Columbia River in present-day Oregon. They built Fort Astoria to protect themselves, but in a ferocious attack by Indians their ship *Tonquin* was sunk. This left them stranded with no supplies or ammunition.

The only way to get help was overland, so a small party set off, led by Robert Stuart. It was dangerous enough living at Fort Astoria with barely enough to keep them safe and alive; it was even more dangerous to go off into the unknown. Their settlement was on the west coast; the only other Europeans were far away beyond the Rocky Mountains. They had to cross almost the whole continent for the first time, with no maps or guides, and few supplies.

Stuart's party built canoes, and managed to buy horses by barter with the Indians. The first part of their trek was through waterless, hilly country. Then the land became flatter, but the heat was overwhelming and there were plagues of mosquitoes. Winter came, and the weather turned bitterly cold. The travelers were starving. They were saved by Shoshoni Indians who provided them with dog meat, dried salmon, and cakes made from roots and berries.

Cheered by this, they set off again following an Indian trail. But their luck did not last. Hostile Crow Indians ran off with their horses, and they had to continue on foot. Even so, they managed to cross the Rockies by way of South Pass. Eventually they reached the Missouri River and St. Louis where a rescue party for the Astorians was soon organized. The first important fur trading post in the Pacific Northwest had been saved, and Stuart had "blazed" from west to east what later became the Oregon Trail.

Trappers lived a harsh life. They had to carry heavy guns, traps, and carcasses through rough, hostile country. Even around the camp fire, they had to be alert to danger.

LIVING WITH THE IROQUOIS

Impressed by his courage, savage Indians twice spared the life of this daring explorer who lived among them and learned their skills.

Pierre Radisson was 15 when his family sailed from France to settle in Canada in 1651. He quickly discovered the excitement of exploring the forest and wilderness along the St. Lawrence near their home. Not many people ventured far outside the settlement for fear of attack by hostile Indians. For by befriending the Huron Indians, the French had become the sworn enemies of the fiercest tribe, the Iroquois.

Capture by Indians

Ignoring the dangers, Pierre Radisson and two friends set off into the forest to go hunting. Pierre was the boldest and went ahead of the other two. Turning back later, he came across the terrifying sight of their bodies, scalped and bristling with arrows. Iroquois Indians had been stalking them and shot them down.

The war party now surrounded Pierre and attacked him. He fought them off with all his might. His attackers were so impressed by his courage and strength that instead of scalping him they took him back to their camp as a prisoner.

He was adopted as one of the tribe and he learned many Indian skills, including the art of tracking and how to build and handle a birch-bark canoe. As a result he became an even better hunter and fisherman. As a young brave, he also grew to understand Indian ways of thinking, so that he could predict their reactions in certain situations.

Undaunted even by the sight of his dead companions, Radisson fought off his Iroquois attackers so bravely that they spared his life.

Escape from the Iroquois

Pierre managed to escape once but was recaptured and brutally tortured for two days. Once again, the Indians were impressed by his courage. Instead of scalping him – the most shameful death for an Indian – they took him back into the tribe and for one more year he lived with them as a painted warrior.

His thorough knowledge of Indian ways was invaluable to him on the expeditions he led later, after finally escaping from the Iroquois. The Indians taught him how to track beaver. To cover their own scent, the hunters waded through icy streams that might turn into rushing torrents at any moment, sweeping them to their death. They lured the beavers into traps by using scent glands cut from the body of another beaver to attract them.

Radisson and Groseilliers

Radisson went back to Montreal where he met his new brother-in-law Sieur Groseilliers. They both shared a keen sense of adventure and an urge to explore their new country. Pierre Radisson was brave, impetuous, and imaginative. Groseilliers, who was much older, was more methodical and cautious in his planning. He was also a good businessman and the

Radisson won respect from an Indian chief by displaying "white man's magic." The Indians were not familiar with explosives – though they soon came to be.

First rendezvous with the Sioux

Radisson and Groseilliers were probably the first Europeans to meet with the Sioux tribe. The Indians had heard that the two Frenchmen were coming and were eager to exchange their furs for metalware, tools, weapons, and jewelry. At first the Sioux pretended to be unimpressed by the travelers' kettles and mirrors, bells and blankets. Radisson guessed what was going on in the minds of the powerful chiefs who stood proudly apart wearing their magnificent war bonnets. Quickly taking a handful of gunpowder he threw it into the fire. The flash and explosion startled and amazed the Indians who held strong beliefs in the powers of magic. Radisson had won their respect and the trading could begin.

Freeze and famine

Radisson and Groseilliers took many risks to procure the long, thick beaver furs. At the end of the season, they loaded all the furs and hides from their catch on to packhorses and sledges. The journey back to the nearest trading post was invariably long and dangerous. Some routes involved crossing frozen lakes where the ice might be dangerously thin as the spring thaw began. The rivers would be swollen with icy water melting from the snow rushing over the rocks and creating treacherous rapids.

One year, while crossing one of the Great Lakes their canoes narrowly missed being crushed by drifting ice floes. They spent the depth of the winter cut off at an Indian camp and almost starved. They survived by eating roots, dogs, and wood. In desperation they gnawed at the beaver skins in the hope of gaining some nourishment.

two of them made an ideal exploration team.

Together they launched several daring expeditions, traveling with Indians from friendly tribes. They canoed across some of the Great Lakes and had to shoot the rapids on the rivers. Where these became impassable they carried, or portaged, their birch-bark canoes overland. They succeeded in penetrating Indian country farther westward and northward than any other Europeans.

At any moment Radisson and Groseillier's fur-laden canoe could have been crushed.

The heroes return

In the spring the two men were thin and exhausted but they managed to get to the Indians' meeting place and trade their manufactured goods for food and more furs. When they returned to Montreal with a flotilla of canoes piled high with furs they were given heroes' welcomes by family and friends. But the French government officers claimed they had been trading without a proper license. Radisson wound up in prison.

The shining water

When he was released from prison, Radisson offered his services to the British. He was not interested in simply becoming rich. He loved the challenge of traveling and exploring and was not to be put off by the threat of his fellow countrymen. The English authorities asked him to lead an expedition to a place he had heard of from the Indians and long wished to see, Hudson Bay, "the shining water which tastes of salt and is so wide you cannot see the far shore." From this successful expedition grew the Hudson's Bay Company.

▫ PILGRIM PIONEERS ▫

When the explorers returned to Europe with tales of the New World there was a race between all the countries waiting to claim land here. But life was not easy for the early settlers.

The first English expedition to the New World was organized by Sir Walter Raleigh in 1585. He established a colony and named it Virginia, after the Virgin Queen, Elizabeth I. The first group of colonists struggled hopelessly against cold, hunger, and disease, and soon returned to England.

A second expedition set out, led by John White whose daughter Virginia was born a month after they landed. White returned to England for more supplies, but England was at war with Spain and it was two years before a ship could be spared to take White back with supplies. He found the fort he had built deserted. Nobody knows whether the settlers died of starvation or were killed or captured by Indians. But the Indians spoke of a "white queen" who lived among them. Was this John White's daughter?

Indian friends and enemies

The first successful colony was founded at Jamestown, largely thanks to the determination of a soldier named John Smith. Hunger, disease, and Indian attacks had demoralized the settlers. But Smith taught them how to defend themselves and benefit from the Indians by trading with them, and procuring enough corn to see them through the winter. Smith loved exploring, and soon mapped much of "New England" so accurately that the government used them.

Smith had many narrow escapes in his life including many clashes with Indians. Once, so he claimed, he fought off 200 of them alone. When he was about to be killed by an Indian chief, the chief's daughter, Pocahontas, bravely threw herself in the way, pleading for his life.

Smith was an immensely strong man and survived illness and injury including serious poisoning and a vicious wound from a stingray. Only after he was badly burned in an explosion on his ship, did he return to England to recover in safety.

The brave Pilgrims

Of all the European settlers, the Pilgrims are the most famous. They belonged to a strict religious sect that had been banned by the Church of England. America was where they could live and worship as they pleased, in peace. They arrived late in the year 1620 after a hard voyage on their ship the *Mayflower*. All they had to eat was what they could fish from the ocean or gather from the trees. Their only shelter was what they could build. They trusted in God and did not despair. They were terrified of the "savage" Indians, but began to trade with them and learned to eat the food they ate. They grew corn and squash and went into the wilderness to capture wild turkeys.

In many later settlements, there was trouble with the Indians. Some of the settlers burned the Indians' corn in an attempt to drive them away, but this only

led to the Indians' starvation and desperation. In 1676, the settlement of Lancaster in Massachusetts was invaded by Nipmuck Indians. They killed 50 people and kidnapped the minister's wife, Mary Rowlandson, and their six-year-old daughter. The house was set on fire.

As the villagers fled, the Indians attacked them with guns, spears, and tomahawks. Mary was carrying her daughter and a bullet struck them both. The Indians forced the wounded pair to go with them into the snowy wilderness. Mary Rowlandson told how they had nothing to eat or drink but a little cold

John Smith is spared the executioner's axe, thanks to the bravery of the Indian princess Pocahontas who risked her life to save his.

water and any nuts, roots, tree bark, or small animals they could catch. After six days the little girl died.

Mary was not used to a harsh life in the wilderness. Desperate with grief, her head felt light and dizzy, her knees weak, and her body raw and sore. Yet she survived captivity for three months, earning her food by making stockings and shirts for the Indians until they released her for a ransom of a few dollars.

□ THE MISSISSIPPI □

The Father of Waters, as the Indians called the great Mississippi River, was the vital link between the steaming bayous on the Gulf of Mexico and the frozen lakes on the frontier with Canada.

The first explorer to reach the Mississippi River was Hernando de Soto, the Spanish leader who was as cruel as he was brave. He found the river in 1542 while searching for the legendary gold of El Dorado. At the same time he hunted down, killed, or kidnapped many Indians. His idea was to sell them in the West Indies as slaves. The Indians took their revenge and murdered him. No white man saw the river again for 100 years.

A peaceful mission
Two French-Canadians, Father Jacques Marquette, a missionary, and Louis Joliet were told of the great river that flowed south through rich hunting country. In 1673 they set out to find it. They ignored warnings that the country was inhabited by ferocious tribes and that a demon lived in the river. The demon's roar could be heard from far off and the waters were known to devour canoes. If they survived these dangers, they would be burned up by the terrible heat.

Unafraid, Marquette and Joliet, and five companions, paddled away in their birch-bark canoes. They crossed Lake Michigan and then traveled southwest on the Fox River. There they met a demon, a monstrous catfish that nearly capsized one boat! The water churned through steep gorges, raced over rapids, and threatened to swallow their flimsy canoes. They carried their canoes across

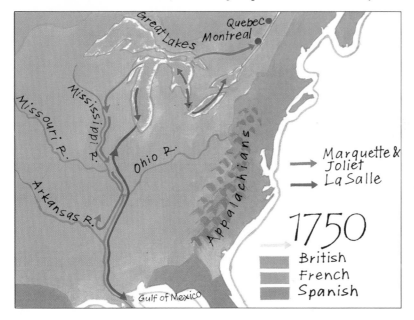

Marquette and Joliet (right) offered peace and Christianity to the Indians they met on their journey down the Mississippi. They turned back rather than enter Spanish territory. La Salle's later expedition went all the way to the Gulf of Mexico. The map (left) shows the routes of both expeditions.

land to the Wisconsin River which flowed into a broad and beautiful river. It was the Mississippi.

Down the Mississippi

Boldly they paddled on downstream for over two weeks without meeting anyone. Then they saw footprints on the bank! Father Marquette saw himself as a messenger sent by God and feared no man. Fortunately, the Illinois Indians that they met were friendly, and they had no cause to fear. But the Illinois warned them about other tribes who tomahawked strangers to death, without hesitation.

Some time later, they saw a huge pair of brightly colored, horned monsters staring down at them from a cliff. Was this the demon? No! It was a rock painting of Indian gods. The Indians were fierce and armed with guns, but seeing Father Marquette's Illinois pipe of peace, they let the travelers pass unmolested. But danger lurked ahead, for immediately they found themselves in a great torrent of yellow mud. They had reached the mouth of the Missouri where the great river pours into the Mississippi. Their light canoes were caught in whirlpools and nearly overturned.

Up the Mississippi

Farther south, they found themselves in marshy, insect-infested swamps. Thinking they had nearly reached the river's mouth, they decided to turn back. Ahead lay certain death from the Spanish, or from Indian tribes armed with guns by the Spanish.

They journeyed back to Canada via the Illinois River, toiling through 42 sets of rapids. When they were within sight of home, just above Montreal, tragedy

La Salle erected a monumental crucifix carved with the fleur-de-lis, *symbol of France.*

struck. Joliet's canoe capsized. Two of his men were drowned, and he lost all his papers and possessions. He had to make maps of the river from memory. Even so the Canadian government, which had sponsored the expedition, was pleased with the result. They had thought that the Mississippi might flow into the Pacific Ocean. They now knew that it must flow into the Gulf of Mexico.

Father Marquette, whose mission was religious not geographical, returned later to live among the Illinois Indians. He founded a mission and spent an extremely cold winter in a cabin on the site of Chicago. He was the first white man to live there. But his health was poor and he died in the spring of 1675.

□ LA SALLE'S FATAL AMBITION □

The news of their discovery was just what the successful fur trader Robert de La Salle had hoped for. He had already explored Lake Michigan and the valley of the Illinois River. It became his dream to win the rich hunting grounds of the Mississippi valley for France. But the only known way to them at present lay through the barren, frozen wastes of Canada which teamed with hostile people, and was barred by ice for half the year. Even so, La Salle braved the journey. He traveled all the way to the river's mouth, and claimed all the land for King Louis of France, to be known as Louisiana. He established a colony of French settlers on the Illinois River.

Not satisfied with these achievements, La Salle returned to France to gain more government backing. He knew that the best way of reaching the Mississippi valley was from the south, not from the north. His plan was to found a colony on the Gulf of Mexico, at the mouth of the river. He sailed back to America with a fleet of four ships carrying provisions, equipment, and 200 colonists.

Conditions were bad on the ships and worse when they landed. La Salle had arrived at the wrong place. The settlement they built was not at the mouth of the river. Determined to find the Mississippi, La Salle forced his men to march overland to find it. But they were harassed by Indians and weakened by disease. La Salle, driven by his own ambition, drove them on. In the end, they could take no more, and they murdered him.

Watched by a horrified friar, La Salle was shot in the head by a disgruntled follower.

□ THE WILDERNESS ROAD □

Daniel Boone, the Kentucky backwoodsman, was renowned for his courage even during his lifetime.

Daniel Boone was born of a Quaker family in Pennsylvania in 1734. He and his brothers and sisters learned to love the wilderness. Their parents had a small farm and Daniel often took care of the cows that were free to roam in the woods. He learned all he could about the trees and animals, and he could recognize the song of the birds and the tracks of every creature. He also learned the ways of the Indians from a friendly tribe that lived nearby.

At 13 he went off hunting alone. Several days later he was found, calmly roasting a bear he had shot and skinned. Once asked if he was ever afraid, he replied, "Fear is the spice that makes it interesting to go ahead."

Kentucky – a hunter's paradise

As a young man, Daniel joined the militia. He heard tales of lands beyond the Appalachian mountains where the buffalo roamed the lush bluegrass meadows. If only he could find this hunter's paradise that the Indians called Ken-take, meaning "great meadow."

When he was 21, Daniel married a neighbor's daughter, Rebecca. Over the years they had nine children. Daniel was often away on long hunting trips, so Rebecca had to guard their cabin, care for the children, and tend their own little farm. She was as fearless as her husband.

Daniel Boone.

In 1769, an old friend suggested an expedition to find Kentucky. Boone could not resist the challenge. He had spent so many years hunting and farming to feed the family. Now it was time for an adventure.

The Warriors' Path

With several more friends, Boone set off. He knew the Indian trail that led to Kentucky. It was the Warriors' Path, a trail used by Indians on the warpath. Dressed in deerskins and moccasins, Boone traveled through the forests and under the towering cliffs of the Cumberland Mountains. The trail wound up and over a low pass – the Cumberland Gap – which was the way west.

The land beyond was a paradise. The soil of the blue plains of Kentucky was rich and fertile, perfect land for farming and for grazing. Deer and buffalo roamed in huge herds and the woodlands were alive with turkeys.

Saving his skin

After two years of exploring, Boone returned home to collect his family. He had found a wonderful new land for them to settle, and he was bringing a fortune in skins that he had risked his life to collect.

Indians raided the travelers' camp and stole all the skins, along with their supplies of ammunition, clothes, and food.

The travelers managed to get away, but the Indians pursued them down the trail and almost had Boone in their grasp. Just in time, he leapt over the edge of a high cliff. The Indians were certain he would be dashed to pieces on the rocks below, but Boone landed in a tree just

With characteristic coolness, Boone stood his ground in the path of a buffalo stampede. At the last possible moment, he shot the leading animal, and pulled his terrified companion to safety behind its body.

over the cliff edge. To the fury of his pursuers, he climbed down and got away.

The Boone family moves west

In 1773, the Boone family and a number of friends set out with all their possessions, eager to reach the new land. But a war party of Cherokee Indians was waiting. They ambushed Boone's teenage son James and his friends. When Boone found them, they were dead, and it was clear from the scalped and mutilated bodies that they had been tortured.

Boone wanted to press on despite the tragedy, but his wife would not hear of it. The party that had set out so bravely decided that no country could be worth such risks, and turned back.

The building of Boonesborough

After years of conflict a treaty was made. The Indians sold the white settlers some land in Kentucky and promised a safe

With her father's skill, young Jemima Boone dupes her Indian captors.

road to reach it. It was Boone who cleared the road – the Wilderness Road. At its end, he built a stockaded settlement for the settlers and called it Boonesborough. Boone was always urging the people to protect themselves for, despite the treaty, hostile Indians often attacked the fort. The Shawnee captured his daughter Jemima along with some friends, thinking they had a great prize. But Jemima knew all about tracking. She left an easy trail for her father to follow so that he could rescue them.

Capture at Blue Licks

An essential requirement for the settlers was salt, which was used to preserve meat. There was a fine saltwater spring at a place called Blue Licks. On an expedition there to make salt, Boone and his companions were captured by Shawnee. The British authorities tried to buy him back but the Indians would not give up their hostage. They took Boone and a few others to live with their tribe. They were immensely proud of their important catch, and Boone cleverly pretended to admire them and their skills. The chief, Blackfish, looked on him as a son.

Eventually Boone escaped and raced back to Boonesborough, in time to warn the settlement of an attack the Shawnee Indians were planning. The fort's occupants prepared for a siege, with stores of food and water, and guns and ammunition ready.

The Indians tried to tunnel into the fort because the walls were strongly defended. They tried to burn it down with flaming arrows. Fires took hold and the settlers had difficulty finding enough water to douse the flames. After ten days, the situation looked hopeless. Then sud-

The Shawnee ceremonially "washed away" Boone's "white blood," plucked out all but a "scalp lock" of his hair, and painted him as a warrior.

denly it began to rain. The fires went out, the tunnel collapsed, and the Indians retreated.

A new life on the Missouri

Although Boone was recognized by all as a clever, courageous leader, he found little reward. His enemies claimed that he had become an Indian spy and he was court-martialed. He was found innocent and returned to his family, but later he had more trouble with the law. It was claimed that he had no title to the land that he had staked out in Kentucky, so he set out for a new wilderness.

At the age of 65 he built a canoe and moved on again to Missouri. There his wife died, and he spent years trying to pay off his debts, even going out hunting over 600 miles of barren country at the age of 80. He died at the age of 86, a lonely but legendary figure.

THE TRAILBLAZERS

In 1803, President Jefferson purchased Louisiana from France. The new territory had to be explored, and the unknown territory beyond it. Two brave men accepted the challenge to blaze a trail all the way to the Pacific and back.

The third President of the United States, Thomas Jefferson, had a dream: one day he would be able to send a scientific expedition to explore the unknown country reaching all the way to the Pacific and establish a route to the west coast that others could follow. That dream came true in 1804, when Meriwether Lewis and William Clark set out together with a party of about 45 people on a journey of 4,000 miles across North America to the Pacific and back.

The members of the expedition were to collect all the scientific information they could about the lands west of the Rockies – its plants and wildlife, rocks and minerals, mountains and rivers – as well as establishing good relations with the different Indian tribes that they met. It was a formidable challenge.

Meriwether Lewis

William Clark

Up the Missouri

Lewis, Jefferson's private secretary, was given the job of organizing and leading the expedition. He asked his former army commander William Clark to join him. After a winter of military training and detailed planning, they started out in May. They traveled up the Missouri in three boats that could be rowed or towed along. In these boats they sur-

vived the terrible torrents of swirling, muddy water that roared down the Missouri after every thunderstorm. On the border of South Dakota they left all known settlements behind them. From now on they were in the wilderness. They were able to shoot some buffalo, which gave them fresh meat to eat and valuable furs to trade. Moments after they had killed them a terrible duststorm stampeded the whole herd.

Winter among the Indians

Continuing up river in torrential rain and storms, disaster almost struck one boat when the riverbank collapsed on it.

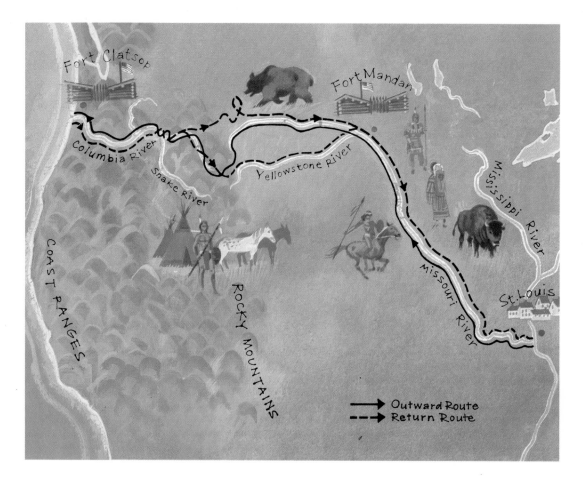

Outward Route
Return Route

Then a war party of dangerous Sioux Indians captured Clark. He calmly demanded to be released, telling them of the important, peaceful mission he was engaged on — and stressing how large and well-armed his expedition was! Wisely the Indians let him go.

By October the expedition was well into what is now North Dakota and the winter gales were beginning. They came to a settled community of Mandan Indians, who farmed and traded with other Indians and white settlers. Lewis and Clark built a winter camp near the settlement. Lewis gave treatment to some of the Indians with the medicines he car-

Lewis and Clark's party left St. Louis on May 14, 1804. They arrived back on September 23, 1806, with an immense fund of information about the land and its people.

ried, including a young woman called Sacagawea, which means bird woman. She was from the Shoshoni tribe and knew of the trails leading westward toward her homeland. She was married to a French-Canadian trapper named Toussaint Charbonneau. The two acted as interpreters and helped to guide the expedition. They traveled with the party for many months, she carrying her baby (papoose) on her back.

Bear country

The party set out again in April and continued up the Missouri into uncharted territory (now Montana). The land was wild and populated by fearsome grizzly bears. Guns had almost no effect on them. One wounded grizzly angrily gave chase to Lewis, who just managed to fire a fatal shot before the bear could maul him. Clark successfully killed an enormous grizzly, but at the same time disturbed another that immediately tore toward him and his companions. They all fired their guns as it approached but it did not stop. The men turned and fled and only escaped the bear's terrible claws by diving over a cliff into the river.

Sacagawea and her baby are saved from swirling floodwaters by Clark and Charbonneau. On another occasion, it was she who saved their precious possessions.

In June the expedition came to the Rocky Mountains and the great waterfalls the Indians had described. To get past the falls they had to carry their canoes with all their equipment for 20 miles overland. The ground was covered with prickly pear cactus, and the spines pierced the soft leather of their moccasins. During this portaging stage there were terrific hailstorms, and mud and rockslides would pour down on them. Once Sacagawea lost her footing in the swirling floodwater. Just in time, Clark saved her and the baby, but much of their equipment was washed away.

Across the Rockies

In the hot, damp climate of the river valley the travelers were plagued with mosquitoes and biting insects that brought disease. Clark became ill with a fever and had a serious leg injury, at times so painful that he could scarcely walk. He refused to give up and struggled on.

The huge mountains seemed an impenetrable barrier even to the experienced frontiersmen of the party. The going was hard. It was hot and they were carrying heavy equipment. They pressed on bravely until they found the Shoshoni tribe they were seeking. Sacagawea was delighted to meet with some of her own people. The Indians sold them horses as pack animals and guided them across the mountains, with Sacagawea acting as interpreter.

They took the Lola trail, a difficult and dangerous path over the Rockies.

Then they crossed the Bitterroot Mountains, portaging the canoes until they reached a westward-flowing stream. This stream was a tributary of the Columbia River that would take them to the west coast.

It was vital for the party to get out of the mountains before the winter freeze gripped them. They built sturdy boats to aid their progress. By November 17 they had passed the Cascade Mountain range and caught sight of the Pacific Ocean. They had reached the far edge of the continent at last.

Winter on the Pacific

The winter on the coast was a bitter disappointment. They built Fort Clatsop to keep out hostile Indians and hostile weather. The weather was constantly

Sweating with fever and plagued by buzzing insects, Clark is nursed by Lewis. Neither man was medically qualified but they coped with the needs of the whole expedition.

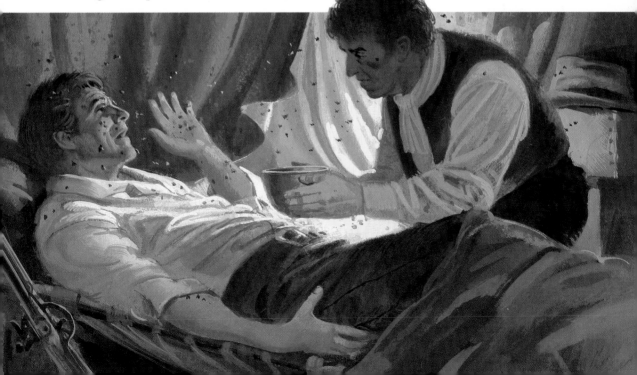

wet and freezing cold. They had very little food as their stock of goods for trading with the Indians had almost run out. They ate mostly fish. With no fresh vegetables, the men became ill. Terrific floods and rockslides threatened to destroy their cabins. Indians stole their horses and supplies. By spring they had almost nothing but their wits to live on.

The struggle home

The party set off on the return journey with only one canoe. They had bought it

Fort Clatsop was misery: the party was cold, wet, and short of food. News of a beached whale sent them hurrying to negotiate with the Indians for a share of its blubber and oil.

in exchange for Lewis's best coat and some tobacco. Desperately in need of food, Clark performed "magic" tricks to impress the Indians by throwing explosives into a fire, and making the flames change color. One friendly tribe gave them ten dogs to take with them to eat. To buy back their horses, they sold buttons cut off spare coats and used Clark's medical skill as a form of barter.

Recrossing the Bitterroot range proved extremely difficult for the horses. There were treacherous icy precipices hanging over rocky ravines and in places the snow was 50 feet deep. Once over the mountains, they found some hot springs where they set up camp to recover their health and strength. Clark built a thermal bath and gave heat treat-

ment to sick and injured members of the party, and also to some Indians.

Once the men were fit again, they attempted to map as much new territory as possible. Lewis took one party up the Marias River and Clark surveyed Yellowstone. It was a great risk, creating two smaller, weaker parties in hostile Indian territory. On Clark's route the horses' hooves became badly damaged by the rough ground, so he had buffalo-hide boots made for them. Lewis was accidentally shot by a poor-sighted companion who thought he was aiming at an elk. In great pain, he lay in a boat for days while the men paddled on to rendezvous with the other party. Clark then removed the bullet from his thigh and dressed the wound.

Given up for dead

On the outward journey they had hidden some of their supplies and many of the plant specimens they had collected in "caches" dug in the ground. When they reached the spot on the return journey they found that it had been flooded. One cache, containing all their plant specimens, was completely ruined but the others were still safe.

There were still dangers ahead including plagues of biting insects and attacks by grizzly bears and Indians. Most people at home had given the party up for dead. In fact only one man had died during the whole expedition – probably of an appendicitis that nobody could treat. When they finally reached St. Louis, they were given a hero's welcome.

□ SPYING OUT NEW LANDS □

Even after Lewis and Clark's achievement, thousands of miles of America were still unmapped and unexplored. The government sent out expeditions to explore and map these unknown areas – and keep an eye on the neighboring Spanish territory.

□ ZEBULON PIKE – SOLDIER SPY □

A mystery surrounds the American soldier and explorer, Zebulon Pike. His work in finding and mapping good routes through the mountains and deserts of the Southwest (while Lewis and Clark were exploring the Northwest), helped the government to claim new lands and showed the way for American immigrants who wanted to move west.

Pike's first expedition set out to search for the source of the Mississippi; the next was to find the source of the Arkansas River and to settle some feuds between warring Indian tribes. In 1806, the party started up the Arkansas River. From far out in the plain, Pike sighted the first massive peak of the Rockies. It was already November, far too late in the year to venture into the mountains, but Pike could not resist the challenge. After three days' struggling through deep snow, in totally unsuitable clothing, Pike abandoned the attempt, but even so— Pikes Peak – was named after him.

Then the party traveled southward, still in the mountains. Progress was slow in the icy conditions. After two weeks the horses were exhausted. Pike decided to abandon them and part of the baggage, leaving them and two of his men in a log shelter. The rest of the party continued the terrible journey. By the time they reached the relative safety of the plains beyond the mountains, they were cold, hungry, and exhausted. Two men lost their feet to frostbite, and six others were crippled with gangrene.

To add to their misery they found that they were in Spanish territory. Pike was arrested on suspicion of spying (which he may have been), although he claimed that they were just lost. He was taken prisoner and sent to various Spanish forts. Eventually he was released and made his way home. Even though all his maps and papers had been taken, he had memorized much of what he had seen and heard. He had also hidden a set of maps inside a gun barrel.

□ JOHN FRÉMONT – PATHFINDER □

John Frémont was an army surveyor who explored much of the area between the Rocky Mountains and the Pacific, and produced the first accurate map of the American West. Like Pike, he was a daredevil, leading his companions across high mountains in midwinter, and acting as an unofficial spy for the government. He was known as the "pathfinder," but mostly he followed known trails. His skill was in describing and recording them so that others could follow. He produced an invaluable guidebook for people taking wagon trains to the West.

Kit Carson and his men follow an Indian trail through the desert. If the water holes and gulleys dried up, the travelers and their horses were likely to meet the same fate as the cattle that starved to death in the blazing sun.

Two of his surveying expeditions took him into the Spanish territory of California. The wary Spanish ordered him to leave. Instead, Frémont boldly climbed Hawk's Peak nearby and hoisted the American flag. To save his men from the Spanish, he organized a retreat to the north under cover of darkness.

When the Mexican War broke out, Frémont led a troop of American volunteers to the victory that gave California to the United States. After the war, Frémont made two attempts to try and find a route across the continent for the railroad. Later, he became a politician and displayed his courage in another field by speaking out boldly against slavery.

◻ KIT CARSON ◻

John Frémont's great friend on many expeditions was the frontiersman Kit Carson, a skillful hunter and daring soldier.

He went with Frémont to the Rocky Mountains, Oregon, and California. His knowledge of Indian trails, his prowess as a hunter, and his fearlessness as a fighter brought him great fame. Carson managed to avoid a clash with the Sioux tribe, the terror of many travelers. He carried reports of their activities to government officials in Washington.

On one of his trips he met a force of Americans going to fight the Mexicans. The commander General Kearny immediately ordered Carson to guide his troops. During one attack, Carson and two others slipped through the enemy lines to get help from San Diego. They had to creep or crawl a lot of the way — nearly 32 miles.

After the war Carson acted as "agent" for the Apaches, and named his horse Apache after them. During the Civil War he fought bravely on the Southern side and was promoted to brigadier general.

37

THE MOUNTAIN MEN

The wild appearance of the mountain men frightened townsfolk. But travelers were grateful for their woodsman's skills and intimate knowledge of the mountains.

When a mountain man rode into town with his load of furs, his wild appearance frightened some of the local residents. He would look quite terrifying with his tanned skin, long unkempt hair, and rough beard sprouting beneath a beaver skin cap. His buckskin pants and hunting shirts were decorated with bristling porcupine quills or leather fringes, and he wore soft, beaded moccasins for silent stalking and hunting. In his wide leather belt was thrust a pistol, a tomahawk,

A typical mountain man.

and a scalping knife with a few gruesome animal skulls dangling down. Always on hand was a big Hawkins rifle.

The mountain men were usually tough characters, total "loners" who traveled through the Rockies, following the faintest trails and forging new routes through the mountains. They lived outdoors, trapping their own meat, and making clothes from skins.

◻ COLTER'S HELL ◻

One of the first mountain men was John Colter. He was a soldier on Lewis and Clark's expedition but left them to go off alone, exploring and trapping. After three years, he came back with such amazing tales of his adventures that few believed him. He told of a place (known later as Colter's Hell) on Stinking Water River where there were bubbling hot springs and steaming geysers reeking of sulfur. He must have been the first white man to see the place that became Yellowstone National Park.

Captured by Blackfoot Indians, Colter's partner was murdered. Then Colter, who had been stripped naked, was challenged to a race — with his life as the prize. After six miles across rock and cactus scrub, he had outrun most of the murderous pursuers. Finally, wrestling with the leader, he snatched his spear and killed him. Then Colter dived into the river and hid under driftwood while the angry Blackfoot searched for him. Several days later he staggered to safety at a trading post and told his tale.

▫ JIM BRIDGER ▫

Jim Bridger joined a fur-trading company before he was 20, and went on to become one of the greatest American frontiersmen. He learned how to track like an Indian, how to wade for miles through icy water so as to leave no scent, and how to lure the beaver with a bundle of twigs smeared with beaver musk. Alone or with others, he blazed many trails through the mountains in search of furs, and in peril from Indians. He was shot by a Blackfoot and the arrowhead stayed embedded in his back for three years. Acting as a guide and scout, the fearless Bridger led many parties of travelers safely through the mountains. He later built Fort Bridger, a staging post where people could rest without fear of attack.

▫ JOSEPH WALKER ▫

Captain Benjamin de Bonneville was a soldier and explorer. For over two years he explored California and the Rocky Mountains. With him went his mountain-man guide Joseph Walker. Together the two men crossed the Sierra Nevada where Walker was the first white to see the peaks of Yosemite. After searching for gold in California, Walker recrossed the mountains through a pass that came to bear his name. Then he set out to hunt down Mangas Coloradas, the deadly chief of the Apache Indians. At the same time he marked what was to become the California Trail.

Joe Walker acted as a guide to de Bonneville. His Indian wife rode with him.

KNIGHT IN BUCKSKIN

A quiet, kindly man with a mission, Jed Smith was called a knight as much for his courtesy as his courage.

Jedediah Smith was not a typical mountain man. He was always clean-shaven, he never smoked, he never swore, and he never got drunk. He took his Bible with him everywhere. He inspired his men with his courage and strong religious faith. He encouraged them not to give up hope when times were hard. They called him the Knight in Buckskin.

The way through the Rockies

Jed wanted to make a living from beaver furs. Along with other mountain men, he endured many a hard winter hunting and trapping, often putting his life at risk in encounters with fierce wild animals like the huge grizzly bears that roamed the Rockies. It was the practice to follow frozen rivers, searching for beaver. At one low pass in the mountains Jed broke the ice on the river and discovered to his amazement that the water flowed westward. He realized that this was a way across the mountains.

Scorching deserts and high sierras

In 1826, Smith led an expedition to explore between the Rockies and California, hoping to establish a trade route. The party left from the Great Salt Lake and traveled through Ute and Paiute ter-

ritory. They crossed the Mojave desert with its terrible, blistering heat and arrived at a friendly mission station in California, which at that time belonged to the Spanish. The governor accused Smith of spying and ordered him to leave.

This time, rather than return the way they had come, Smith attempted to cross the high Sierra Nevada range. His party faced snow and ice and bitterly cold winds. They struggled on only to meet with the searing heat of the Nevada desert. In the hottest part of the day they buried themselves up to the neck in sand. They tried to slake their thirst by chewing the cabbage pear cactus. Horses died,

food supplies ran out, and they faced death. One man lay down to die but Smith struggled on until they found water and then staggered back with some to save him.

Comanche attack

When the travelers met up with their friends at last, they learned that they had been given up for dead. Despite this terrible ordeal, Smith returned to California the following year. This time ten of his men were killed by Indians. Smith managed to escape but he did not give up exploring. He went north the following year and once again lost many men.

Jed Smith came upon a grizzly bear, wounded and angry. The beast tore his scalp, ripped away his ear, and broke several of his ribs. His companion killed the bear and sewed up Jed's wounds with ordinary thread.

When he was only 32, Smith joined a wagon train that was following the Santa Fe trail. In a search for water he met with a group of Comanche Indians armed with muskets and lances. Smith was alone. He put up a heroic fight and shot their chief. They killed him in a frenzy and threw his body into a ravine to be picked clean by wild dogs and birds. The story became a Comanche legend.

□ MOVING WEST □

After the trailblazers, pathfinders, and frontiersmen came the pioneers.
These were ordinary people with the courage to follow in the footsteps of the great explorers, and explore new territory for themselves.

The Oregon Trail

For the pioneers, reaching the rich western lands of Oregon in the north and California in the south, meant at last finding a place to make a home — and perhaps a fortune. The way to the west lay over tremendously long and difficult trails cut through wilderness, prairies, and deserts, and across the great backbone of the Rockies. The longest of all was the Oregon Trail, an 1,800 mile journey that tested the faith, strength, and courage of all who followed it. The pioneers had a host of different reasons for braving the five-month journey.

Disease, wild animals, and Indians brought death to many. Cruel accidents such as drowning in flash floods took their toll as well. Often they had to endure freezing temperatures, and food and water shortages.

The first wagon train to set out on the Oregon Trail was led by William Sublette in 1830. Ten small wagons stocked with supplies left St. Louis together with 80 men riding mules along the rough trail. On the way, the steep banks of the North Platte River had to be dug away to allow the wagons to pass. Sublette later explored new routes and found a short cut – Sublette's Cutoff – that made the journey shorter for those who followed. The door to the west was South

Pass, a gap in the great Rocky Mountain chain through which wagons could pass. It was about half way along the trail. From here the trail turned north along the Snake River to Walla Walla and then west along the Columbia River.

The settlers would never have reached Oregon safely without the help of frontiersmen like Wild Bill Hickok. He was

a tremendously strong man with such great skill and courage that he could fight a bear or hold off a band of outlaws single-handed, although he never killed anyone except in self-defense. After serving with the army he became a stagecoach driver on the Oregon Trail, also acting as scout and peace officer to prevent Indian attack.

Thousands braved the hardships of the Oregon Trail, their hopes, families, and belongings crammed into covered wagons.

The Gold Rush

In 1848 gold was discovered in California and a great rush began. One hundred thousand people poured into California. Few found gold but many settled as farmers. In 1869 the first transcontinental railroad was completed. By this time almost the whole of North America was settled. There was still much to explore in so vast and wild a country but life had become easier. The men who braved the wilderness had made it possible for a great nation to develop.

□ PEOPLES AND PLACES □

Apache Indians Fearsome Southwest tribe. Lived by hunting and raiding.

Arctic Area above Arctic Circle explored by Martin Frobisher, Samuel Hearne, John Franklin, Robert Peary, and Lincoln Ellsworth among others.

Astoria Fort established by fur traders on Pacific coast of Oregon, and named after John Jacob Astor who established it.

Aztecs People of Mexico in Central America conquered by Spanish leader Cortes.

Brendan voyages Possible Atlantic crossing achieved by Irish monks under leadership of St. Brendan in the sixth century A.D.

Canada The part of the North American continent between the Great Lakes and the Arctic Ocean. First claimed by the French but won by the British in 1763.

Cherokee Indians Forest Indians of the southeast.

Comanche Indians Ferocious plains Indians of Southwest who terrorized travelers along the

Cortes conquers Mexico; the Aztecs were easy victims for his well-armed horse troops.

Santa Fe trail.

Coureurs de bois Daring French-Canadian adventurers who went alone into Indian country to trap and trade in furs.

Crow Indians Plains Indians encountered by Stuart on crossing from Astoria to St. Louis.

Cumberland Gap Low pass in Cumberland Mountain range where the "Wilderness Trail" crossed the mountains to reach the rich, fertile plains of Kentucky.

El Dorado Legendary city where gold could be found in abundance. Searched for by Spanish explorers.

Frontiersmen and women People like Kit Carson, Buffalo Bill, William Sublette, Calamity Jane, and Wild Bill Hickok who lived courageous lives in the frontier towns of the "Wild West."

Gold Rush Race to find gold in California after the discovery of gold in 1848.

Grand Canyon Huge gorge cut through Arizona desert by Colorado River. Discovered by Spanish expedition led by Coronado.

Great Lakes A series of large freshwater lakes along border between the United States and Canada named Superior, Michigan, Huron, Erie, and Ontario.

Great Salt Lake Enormous inland saltwater lake in Utah. Region became center of the Mormon religious settlements.

Hudson Bay Huge bay on the northern coast of Canada, leading to Arctic Ocean. Named after English Arctic explorer Henry Hudson.

Huron Indians One of the eastern forest tribes who helped the European settlers to survive in their new land.

Incas People of Peru in South America, conquered by Spanish led by Pizarro.

Iroquois Indians Tribe of the eastern forests, who lived by farming and hunting. They built *long houses* which were tribal dwellings.

Louisiana Territory Vast area of land stretching westward from the Mississippi valley. First claimed for France by La Salle and named after King Louis. Later exchanged in treaties between British, French, and Spanish. Much of it finally sold to United States in the Louisiana Purchase of 1803.

Mandan Indians Plains Indians who were among the first to become settled farmers and traders. Gave shelter to Lewis and Clark's expedition.

Sir Walter Raleigh lands in Virginia; the local inhabitants bow to his superior fire power.

Missionaries Religious leaders who bravely traveled into new territory to convert the Indians to Christianity. Among them were Marquette, Hennepin, Marcus and Narcissa Whitman (who gave medical and spiritual help to settlers on the Oregon Trail), and Brigham Young (leader of the Mormon settlers at Salt Lake City).

Mississippi-Missouri Two great rivers that together provide the key to the north-south route from the Canadian frontier to the Gulf of Mexico. La Salle's expedition was the first to travel the entire length.

Mongols People who traveled by land bridge to America from Eurasia some 40,000 years ago and settled throughout the Americas. They were the forebears of native Americans.

Mountain men Tough group of trappers and fur traders who roamed the west in the early 1800s, meeting up at an annual summer rendezvous to sell their furs to the dealers from the east. They blazed many of the trails across the prairies and through the Rockies. Later some acted as guides or scouts on the wagon trains that followed the trails west. They include Jim Bridger, Jed Smith, John Colter, and Joseph Walker.

Niagara Falls Huge waterfalls on U.S.-Canadian border connecting Lakes Erie and Ontario.

Northwest Passage The "short-cut" to China many Europeans hoped to find around the north of the American continent.

Pacific Northwest Land west of the Rockies and north of California which became known as Oregon Territory. First explored by Lewis and Clark on their descent of the Columbia River during their great transcontinental expedition.

Pilgrims Religious sect members who sailed to the New World on the *Mayflower* to found peaceful settlements and escape religious persecution in Europe. Founded Plymouth colony.

Puritans Strict religious group of settlers from England who founded Boston, Massachusetts Bay Colony in 1630.

Rocky Mountains Great range of mountains stretching the length of North America from the Mexican desert to Alaska.

St. Louis Important trading post on Mississippi River. Starting point of Lewis and Clark's expedition. Now the principal city of Missouri.

Shawnee Indians Forest Indians of the southeast. Daniel Boone was adopted by them.

Shoshoni Indians Indians of California and intermountain region. They befriended Lewis and Clark and acted as guides through the mountains.

Sierra Nevada High mountain range in eastern California.

Sioux Indians Plains Indians of Dakota, renowned as warriors. First encountered by Pierre Radisson.

South Pass The "door to the west." A low crossing place in the formidable Rocky Mountain range which enabled wagon trains to cross the continent from the east to California and Oregon.

Spanish conquistadors Spanish explorers who invaded and conquered parts of Central and

The dashing frontiersman and marshall Wild Bill Hickok was murdered in 1876.

South America. Among them were Cortes in Mexico, Pizarro in Peru, Orellana on the Amazon, De Soto in Florida, and Coronado in the southwestern desert.

Trails Paths, tracks, and passes once used by the Indians became regular routes for travelers crossing the continent to settle in the west. Among them were the Oregon Trail from Missouri to Oregon via South Pass; the California Trail from South Pass; the Spanish Trail and the Santa Fe Trail to southern California.

Ute and Paiute Indians Tribes of California and intermountain region.

Vikings Seafarers who traveled to America in the early eleventh century A.D. and settled briefly in Newfoundland. They included Eric the Red and Leif Ericsson.

Virginia Name given to region of first English settlements by Sir Walter Raleigh in honor of his patron the Virgin Queen Elizabeth I.

Yellowstone Region of hot sulfur springs and geysers in Wyoming. Called "Colter's Hell" after John Colter's tales about their discovery.

EXPLORING NORTH AMERICA

1492 Christopher Columbus made the first of four voyages to the West Indies and Caribbean

1497 John Cabot sailed across the North Atlantic to Canada

1499 Amerigo Vespucci sailed to the West Indies and South America

1508 Sebastian Cabot sailed to North America

1513 Balboa crossed Panama to the Pacific

1520 Ferdinand Magellan discovered the Straits of Magellan

1521 Hernan Cortes overwhelmed the Aztecs in Mexico

1524 Giovanni da Verrazano explored the North American coast

1533 Francisco Pizarro conquered the Incas in Peru

1535 Jacques Cartier explored the St. Lawrence

1539 Hernando de Soto reached the Mississippi

1540 Francisco de Coronado traveled through the American southwest

1541 Francisco de Orellana found the mouth of the Amazon

1585 Walter Raleigh led a colonizing expedition to Virginia

1603 Samuel de Champlain explored the St. Lawrence and the Great Lakes

1608 Champlain founded Quebec

1610 Henry Hudson reached Hudson Bay

1620 Pilgrims sailed to New England in the *Mayflower*

1624 Colony of Virginia founded

1660 Pierre Radisson and Médard des Groseilliers explored the Great Lakes

1673 Jacques Marquette and Louis Joliet explored the Mississippi

1679 Daniel Duluth explored Lake Superior and the Upper Mississippi

1679 Louis Hennepin explored the Great Lakes with Robert de La Salle

1682 La Salle reached the mouth of the Mississippi with Henri de Tonti and Hennepin

1731 Pierre de la Vérendrye began exploration of the area around Lake Winnipeg with his sons

1754-63 French and Indian War

1759 British captured Quebec

1769 Daniel Boone discovered the Cumberland Gap and the Wilderness Road to Kentucky

1772 Samuel Hearne reached the Arctic Ocean

1776 Declaration of Independence

1783 Treaty of Paris; United States' independence recognized

1789 Alexander Mackenzie reached the Arctic Ocean on the Mackenzie River

1793 Mackenzie reached the Pacific Ocean by way of the Peace River

1803 Louisiana Purchase

1804 Meriwether Lewis and William Clark begin transcontinental expedition

1806 Zebulon Pike explored the midwest and the Rockies

1811 Robert Stuart blazed the Oregon trail eastward from Fort Astoria

1824 Jim Bridger reached the Great Salt Lake

1825 William Ashley explored Utah

1826 Jed Smith blazed a trail across the Rockies to California

1840 John Frémont explored the American west

1841 Settlers took the Oregon Trail to the west

□ INDEX □

48